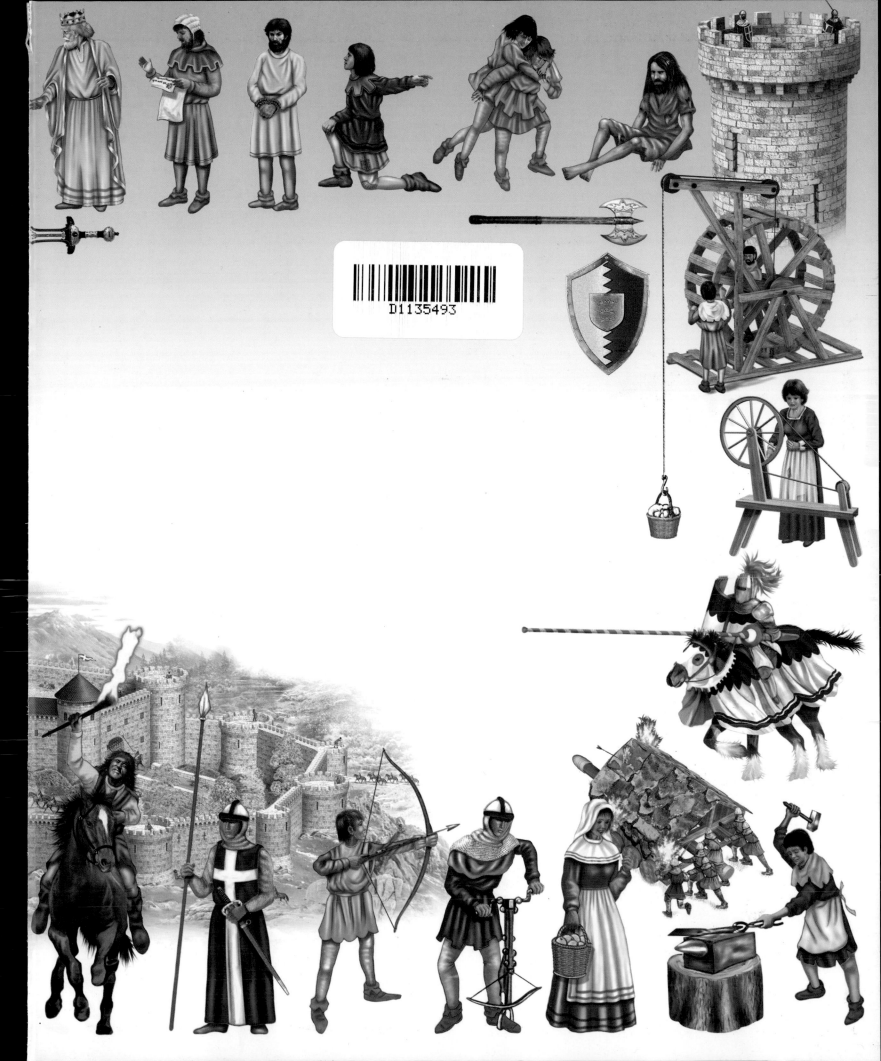

D1135493

© SUSAETA EDICIONES, S.A.
Editor in Chief: Ana Doblado
Original Spanish Text: Francisca Valiente/ Susaeta editorial team
Illustrations: Francisca Valiente
Production: Antonia Maria Martinez
Art Editor: José de Haro

ISBN: 978-0-7097-1867-3
© 2009 Brown Watson, English edition

English edition translated from the
Spanish by Scott Barker

MEDIEVAL CASTLES

Brown Watson

ENGLAND

VILLAGE UNDER ATTACK!

Human beings have always been in constant danger. They had to protect themselves against wild animals, from wars between villages over humble riches, and, of course, against the feared raiders, who had no mercy for anybody or anything.

These raiders stole everything they found of value: food, farm animals, horses and the few everyday weapons and items of jewellery that you might find in poor villages.

There are 4 objects here that would not have existed in Medieval times. Can you find them?

After an attack, those who were still alive had to search for somewhere safer to live with the little they had left or had managed to hide. These people were able to save 7 cows. Can you see them?

The attackers had no respect for anyone, not even women and children. The only thing they could do was run, and if they were lucky, escape.

THE FIRST FORTRESSES

The attacks on hamlets and villages meant that the people had no alternative but to protect themselves, for example, by building walled villages into the sides of hills. They also protected themselves by digging a moat around the wall, or by looking for a place surrounded by water, which would deny access to invaders. Access to the outside world was via a drawbridge, which could be hoisted up when necessary.

There are 9 animals which are not birds or domestic animals. Can you see them? What they could not grow, rear or make in the settlement, they bought from travelling traders. Find 2 donkeys and 10 horses.

There were farms within the fortified enclosure where people reared all types of animals. This meant they bought as little as possible from the outside world.

Can you find 3 swans?

They kept a lookout day and night from the highest towers of the fortress, keeping a careful eye on their territory. A cockerel has escaped from this watchman and he can't find it. Can you see it?

People learned to construct houses that were much stronger and more comfortable than the old straw huts.

If the watchmen saw the slightest danger, they hoisted up the drawbridge to stop any raiders from getting into the fortress. Can you see another bridge?

You'll reach very high if you can find 5 more ladders!

They had to cut down whole forests to build a fortress. Luckily there was plenty of wood at that time. The builders have lost 4 axes! Can you see them?

CONSTRUCTION

The building of a castle involved an awful lot of work and took many years to complete. For security, most castles were built on the top of a hill, but if one was built on level ground, they tried to dig the defensive moat as deep as possible. Hundreds of workers took part in the building work, most of them working in exchange for food.

The stone blocks had to be absolutely level for the whole structure to stay up. Can you find 4 people checking the level of the building?

There are 4 people and 1 object from today's emergency services helping with the construction. Can you find them?

To lift heavy objects, they used a treadwheel crane, which one or two people could climb inside in order to make the wheel turn, just like hamsters do. Try and find 5 more treadwheels.

Cranes with winches were more manageable. They wound the rope with one turn of the handle to lift up or let down the load. Find 4 more.

10

A moat was dug all around the castle to stop enemies scaling the walls and entering the fortress.

Two jobs were indispensable in the construction of a castle: a carpenter, to make the scaffolding, and a blacksmith, who made bars, railings and bolts as well as other items for the security of the castle. They have each lost one of their tools; can you find them?

11

A GREAT CASTLE

Castles were becoming more and more secure. Some had double walls; if the enemy managed to get past the first, they would come up against another fortress inside that was smaller and easier to defend. If this fell too, the king and the all the troops would gather in the main tower and try to defend what was left of the castle from there.

The king is wearing a green cape. Can you see him?

Most castles had a **chapel** or **church**, where all sorts of ceremonies were performed. Can you find another person praying?

The lookout towers were accessed by **spiral staircases**; sometimes they were so narrow that it was difficult to climb them holding a shield and weapons.

The soldiers were able to keep watch over a large area of land from the turret of the main tower thanks to its great height.

There is one knight with a shield and a lilac cape. Where is he?

The rooms in the central tower were the most comfortable in the whole castle.

Castles with double walls had two sets of doors. Each had a drawbridge in case the enemy managed to break through the first. Find 16 horses around the castle.

There are 8 guards with spears dressed in red. Can you see them all?

The dungeons were hidden in the very depths of the tower. Some prisoners, fed only on bread and water, never came out until they died of old age, hunger or illness.

Guards! 4 prisoners have escaped! See if you can find them.

13

THE PARTS OF A CASTLE

The nobles of the castle lived in the central tower, which was called the keep. The servants and cooks were on the ground floor; the first floor housed the royal guard and the armoury; on the floor above was the dining hall where feasts were held; and on the top floor were the living quarters of the nobles.

Look for 1 object on each of the 5 floors that did not exist at the time.

Can you see 23 shields?

When the enemy entered the castle they trapped them by closing the two portcullises.

Can you see the king and queen?

The soldiers threw stones and boiling oil down onto them through the holes in the roof

Entrances were built into the centres of towers, but later they realised that entrances between two towers could be better defended.

This drawbridge was lifted up using a counterweight; to let it down they pulled the chains upwards.

There is one person praying. Can you see him?

This bridge was based on a crankshaft mechanism with chains. This system allowed for bigger and heavier bridges.

14

In the turrets, soldiers were protected from enemy arrows, giving them time to load their bows.

Arrows could be shot from inside the castle, although the narrow opening made it a little difficult to hit the target.

Find 3 archers like this one.

There are 4 soldiers practising their sword fighting, but where are they?

The living quarters of the castle garrison were well guarded by sentries.

Weapons were kept in the towers, and soldiers kept watch so that they were well prepared if the enemy approached.

2 people are practising wrestling. Where are they?

THE PEOPLE

There were laws in the Middle Ages. Anyone who did not obey them had to see their lord or king about it. If anybody committed a very serious crime, they were imprisoned and judged by the king himself, although in most cases the local bailiffs took the law into their own hands.

Keep your eye on the dogs because 4 cats have come in! Can you spot them before the dogs do?

Because it was so difficult to identify knights with their helmets on, they were recognised by the patterns on their shields. See if you can find one of each design.

The royal guard was made up of the most faithful and best-prepared soldiers and noblemen of all the king's armies.

The church was very important at this time. No castle was without a chapel and, of course, a chaplain. Find 6 crucifixes like the one he has in his hand.

The whole royal family lives in the palace accompanied by their servants, the royal guard, chambermaids and all the people most trusted by the king.

Can you see 5 baskets of food?

16

This knight has lost 3 swords. Can you find them?

Before being knighted, noblemen had to first work as pages and squires, serving other knights.

This chamberlain is looking for 10 gold coins! Can you find them?

The chamberlain kept a very tight control over the king's assets. As there were no banks, money was kept under lock and key with guards at the door.

Find 5 yarns of wool.

Most women learnt to sew or spin. Their spinning wheels twisted the wool and formed it into threads of yarn.

17

TOURNAMENTS AND FESTIVALS

In times of peace, the nobles and knights enjoyed themselves by organising festivals. Above all they loved tournaments and jousting. Two knights raced towards each other and tried to knock each other off their horses with lances. Some knights ended up seriously injured, or even dead, from these "games".

This knight is training with a spinning device called a quintain, which has a sack on one end.

Archery was very common at the tournaments.

There are 6 ferocious animals that don't belong here, can you find them?

There are 20 lances and spears in total, can you count them all?

These two are so bad with a bow that they've lost 5 arrows. Can you find them?

Sometimes a knight's armour was so damaged, it had to be repaired immediately.

This knight has been so badly hurt that his squire has to help him.

A knight with his squire awaiting his turn.

There were also wrestling competitions.

If the knight doesn't have quick reflexes, the sack will hit him in the head as it spins round, and could knock him off his horse.

There are 9 swords in total, including these two.

Knights took their practice so seriously that sometimes people got hurt.

Knights trained from a very young age, mounted on a wooden horse that was pulled along by two servants.

Find 4 squires helping their knights.

Although the games were for entertainment, some knights were fatally wounded.

The knight that lost the tournament lost his horse, his weapons, and his honour!

A wooden fence separated the two participants.

The crowd cheered the riders.

A GRAND BANQUET

When there was an important event, the lord of the castle celebrated by holding a great feast and inviting the most important people from the local area. No expense was spared at these banquets, so that everything would go perfectly.

Not only did they cook exquisite delicacies, but they also coloured the food with sandalwood, parsley and saffron to make it look more attractive.

3 platters of fis and 7 dessert have alread been served. Ca you find them all

The juggler has lost 5 batons! Can you help him look for them?

Whole calves were spit roasted for the banquet and then carved and served to the dinner guests. At least the person whose turn it was to rotate the spit would not get cold that night.

3 piglets have managed to escape. Where are they?

The pots they used for cooking were enormous; they had to use a large stick to stir the food.

There are 4 bowls of this stew. Who is going to eat them?

Carts full of food came from outside the castle to supply the kitchen.

5 hens have escaped. Find them!

It was important not to run out of **wine** at these banquets, where people ate until they could eat no more.

This wine merchant has already delivered 3 barrels. Try and find them in the dining hall.

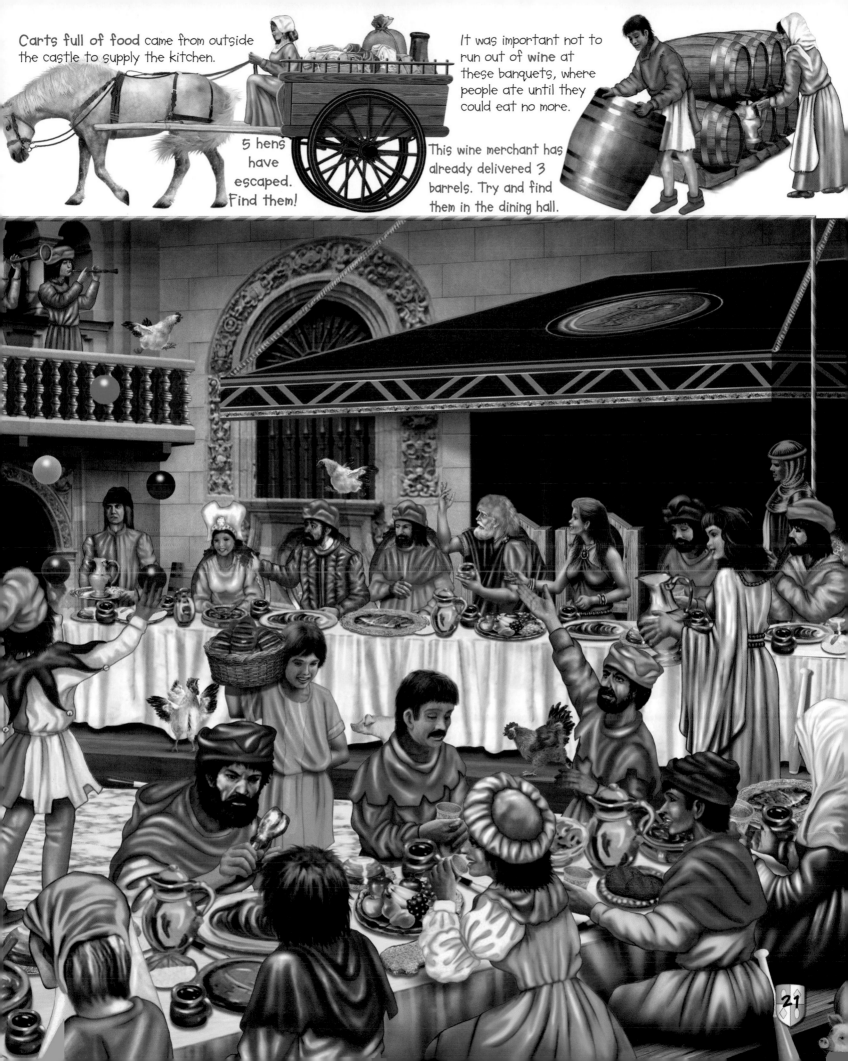

21

LIFE IN THE VILLAGES

The people who lived in the villages near the castle cultivated the land and reared animals in order to obtain food that they could use to pay their lord, who was also the owner of the land and houses. Sometimes the peasants would revolt when taxes, hunger or illness made life impossible for them.

The fields were plots of land that the lord rented to the peasants. They paid him with a share of what they made.

Find 4 shops, which couldn't have sold the products on their signs!

This farmer is going to pay his lord with 9 chickens, 4 geese and a basket of 3 cabbages, but he's lost them! Help him to find everything.

It was the adults who did the hard work of ploughing, but boys worked from a very young age, feeding the animals, clearing the land, leading the sheep and goats to pasture. Girls helped with the household chores.

22

The wooden hoop from a barrel, some wooden stilts, or a hobbyhorse could provide entertainment for these children.

They had everything they needed in the village; everybody sold or exchanged what they produced. Artisans sold what they made.

Find 5 baskets of bread.

Making wooden barrels was an important job as they were used to preserve food.

Look for 6 children playing with these toys.

Counting these two, there are 15 wooden barrels. Watch out, the one on the sign doesn't count!

23

A MEDIEVAL FAIR

Today is a holiday, and the castle has been transformed into one big market. There are all sorts of things to be found here: craftsmen, blacksmiths and carpenters who are mending cart wheels and fixing horseshoes. The castle grounds fill up with traders, advertising their wares in loud voices.

How scary! There are 3 animals that are neither domestic nor from the farm. Can you find them?

The youngsters worked as apprentices, helping their employers with the simplest tasks in order to learn their trade. This apprentice has lost 5 wheels. Can you help him?

The iron was heated in the forge until it was red hot to make it soft and easy to cast or reshape with minimal effort. What a scatterbrain! This blacksmith has lost 6 pairs of tongs. Can you help him find them?

Blacksmiths made or mended railings, horseshoes, carriages, wheels, windows etc. They were useful for almost everything. Find 4 water butts like this one.

Large clay pots were used for storing food.

Traders sold all types of vegetables.

Farmers brought their carts to the fair overflowing with fruit and vegetables to sell. Can you find one basket of eggs?

All types of farm animals were sold or traded at the fair. Try and find at least one of each.

Stallholders sold all sorts of utensils made from copper, silver, metal and clay.

There was often a juggler to liven things up at the fair.

A soldier is keeping watch from a tower to see that there is no trouble at the fair.

People are crowding round this pen full of lambs.

THE CASTLE UNDER ATTACK

The leader of an army had to plan an attack on a castle very carefully. He had to study the lie of the land, the weak points of the fortress, whether it would be easy to surround with his army, and which weapons it would be best to use. If it was not an easy castle to assault, the army would lay siege until the inhabitants either died of hunger or thirst, or surrendered!

One man's bottom is on fire! Can you see him?

The crossbow was a very slow weapon to load, but it could shoot arrows over a great distance.

Soldiers defending the castle pushed the ladders with hooks, so the enemy fell from as high as possible.

Boiling oil or tar was poured from the castle.

There are 11 crossbows including these two. Can you find them?

The stones of the castle itself were used for hurling at the enemy.

Find 6 more ladders.

This spoon shaped catapult could be used to hurl many stones at a time.

Wooden shields were used for protection.

The catapult, with its large counterweight, hurled enormous rocks at high speed.

The enemy filled in the moat with earth so that they could break down the gate with a battering ram.

Attacking soldiers made a tunnel under the castle wall, then set fire to the supports so the walls would collapse.

26

There were double-edged axes.

They cut in both directions!

The swords were highly decorated.

The spikes on this weapon could pierce an iron helmet.

This mace had a ball with spikes.

They made arrows into torches that would set light to the enemy's wooden armaments as they struck.

Try and find 5 arrows with a strange blue flame!

The wooden parapets were protected with wet animal skins to make it more difficult to set them alight.

They swam across the moat to get into the castle through the holes made by the rocks.

They burnt the wooden tower from above to stop the enemy from climbing up.

THE CASTLE IN RUINS

After a big battle, castles were sometimes so badly damaged that neither army could use them. In time, with nobody looking after them, abandoned castles soon fell into disrepair. Today, there are many castle ruins, which would unfortunately be too costly to rebuild.

There are 5 wolves prowling around here. Look for them!

Peasants **helped themselves to stones** to build or improve their homes, which contributed even more to the destruction of the castle.

You can still see where the **2 drawbridges** would have been positioned.

Wooden beams made good loot for restoring the houses in the villages nearest to the castle. **Can you see 6 villagers collecting beams?**

6 eagles are trying to nest in the ruins of this castle. Can you see them?

Simple arrow slit.

Cross-shaped.

Cross-shaped with canon port.

Swans used to swim in the castle moat, before it dried up.

Can you find 8?

There are not many castle ruins where the wall and ceiling decorations can still be seen because, exposed to the open air, they deteriorated very easily.

The slits from where soldiers shot the arrows can still be seen in the ruins of castles.

7 deer are wandering around the ruins at their leisure. Can you find them?